Tic Tac

layers: 2

yers take turns in marking squares on a 3 x 3 grid.
e first player to get three squares in a row wins.

escription

ne player is 'O' and the other is 'X'.

yers take turns in drawing their symbol in one of the cells.
e first player to make a line of three of their symbol horizontally,
rtically, or diagonally wins.

ooth players play perfectly the outcome is always a draw,

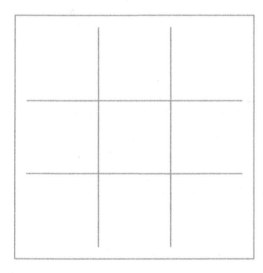

Battleship

Players: 2

Players take turns in trying to guess the locations of the other player's ships on a grid.

Description

Each player's fleet consists of the following ships:

1 × Aircraft Carrier - 5 squares
1 × Battleship - 4 squares
1 × Cruiser - 3 squares
1 × Destroyers - 2 squares
1 × Submarines - 3 square
Each ship occupies a number of adjacent squares on the grid, horizontally or vertically.

Play

During play the players take turns is making a shot at the opponent, by calling out the coordinates of a square (eg A2). The opponent responds with "hit" if it hits a ship or "miss" if it misses. If the player has hit the last remaining square of a ship the opponent must announce the name of the ship; eg "You sank my battleship".

During play each player should record their opponent's shots on the top grid, and their shots on the bottom grid as "X" for a hit and "O" for a miss:

Play

The first player to lose all their ships loses the game.

OPPONENT'S SHIPS

A
B
C
D
E
F
G
H
I
J

1 2 3 4 5 6 7 8 9 10

Aircraft Carrier
AAAAA

Battleship
BBBB

Cruiser
CCC

Submarine
SSS

Destroyer
DD

MY SHIPS

A
B
C
D
E
F
G
H
I
J

1 2 3 4 5 6 7 8 9 10

Aircraft Carrier
AAAAA

Battleship
BBBB

Cruiser
CCC

Submarine
SSS

Destroyer
DD

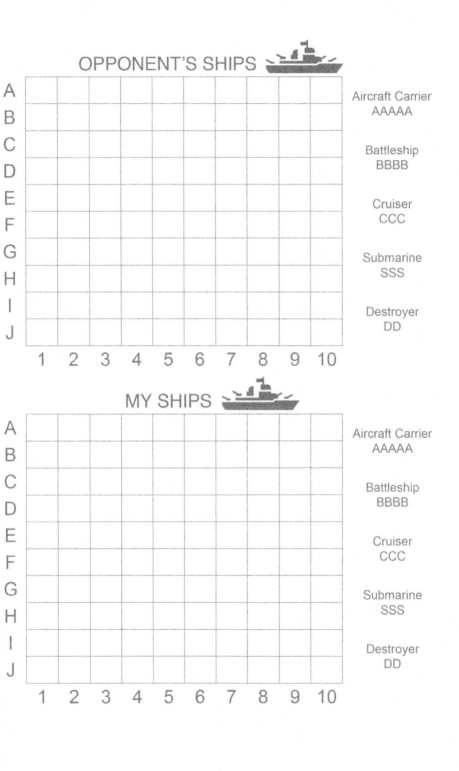

OPPONENT'S SHIPS

	1	2	3	4	5	6	7	8	9	10
A										
B										
C										
D										
E										
F										
G										
H										
I										
J										

Aircraft Carrier
AAAAA

Battleship
BBBB

Cruiser
CCC

Submarine
SSS

Destroyer
DD

MY SHIPS

	1	2	3	4	5	6	7	8	9	10
A										
B										
C										
D										
E										
F										
G										
H										
I										
J										

Aircraft Carrier
AAAAA

Battleship
BBBB

Cruiser
CCC

Submarine
SSS

Destroyer
DD

OPPONENT'S SHIPS

Aircraft Carrier
AAAAA

Battleship
BBBB

Cruiser
CCC

Submarine
SSS

Destroyer
DD

MY SHIPS

Aircraft Carrier
AAAAA

Battleship
BBBB

Cruiser
CCC

Submarine
SSS

Destroyer
DD

OPPONENT'S SHIPS

	1	2	3	4	5	6	7	8	9	10
A										
B										
C										
D										
E										
F										
G										
H										
I										
J										

Aircraft Carrier
AAAAA

Battleship
BBBB

Cruiser
CCC

Submarine
SSS

Destroyer
DD

MY SHIPS

	1	2	3	4	5	6	7	8	9	10
A										
B										
C										
D										
E										
F										
G										
H										
I										
J										

Aircraft Carrier
AAAAA

Battleship
BBBB

Cruiser
CCC

Submarine
SSS

Destroyer
DD

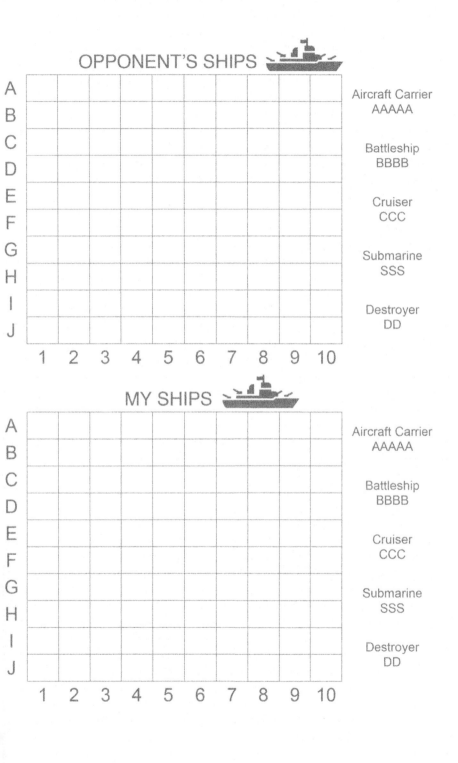

OPPONENT'S SHIPS

	1	2	3	4	5	6	7	8	9	10
A										
B										
C										
D										
E										
F										
G										
H										
I										
J										

Aircraft Carrier
AAAAA

Battleship
BBBB

Cruiser
CCC

Submarine
SSS

Destroyer
DD

MY SHIPS

	1	2	3	4	5	6	7	8	9	10
A										
B										
C										
D										
E										
F										
G										
H										
I										
J										

Aircraft Carrier
AAAAA

Battleship
BBBB

Cruiser
CCC

Submarine
SSS

Destroyer
DD

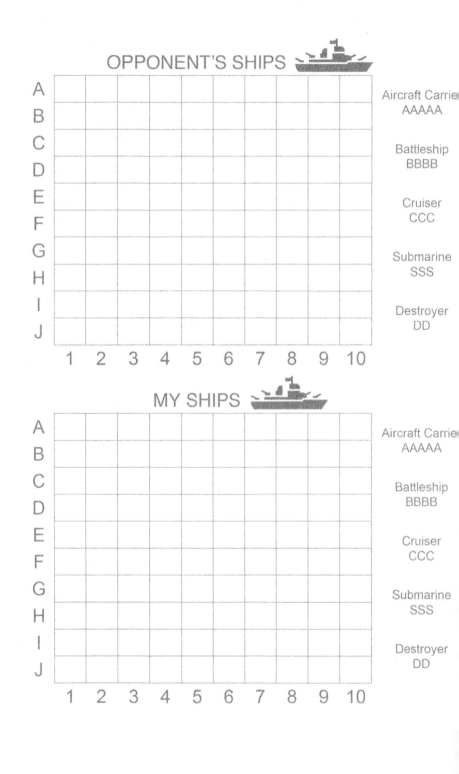

OPPONENT'S SHIPS

	1	2	3	4	5	6	7	8	9	10
A										
B										
C										
D										
E										
F										
G										
H										
I										
J										

Aircraft Carrier
AAAAA

Battleship
BBBB

Cruiser
CCC

Submarine
SSS

Destroyer
DD

MY SHIPS

	1	2	3	4	5	6	7	8	9	10
A										
B										
C										
D										
E										
F										
G										
H										
I										
J										

Aircraft Carrier
AAAAA

Battleship
BBBB

Cruiser
CCC

Submarine
SSS

Destroyer
DD

OPPONENT'S SHIPS

	1	2	3	4	5	6	7	8	9	10
A										
B										
C										
D										
E										
F										
G										
H										
I										
J										

Aircraft Carrier
AAAAA

Battleship
BBBB

Cruiser
CCC

Submarine
SSS

Destroyer
DD

MY SHIPS

	1	2	3	4	5	6	7	8	9	10
A										
B										
C										
D										
E										
F										
G										
H										
I										
J										

Aircraft Carrier
AAAAA

Battleship
BBBB

Cruiser
CCC

Submarine
SSS

Destroyer
DD

OPPONENT'S SHIPS

Aircraft Carrier
AAAAA

Battleship
BBBB

Cruiser
CCC

Submarine
SSS

Destroyer
DD

MY SHIPS

Aircraft Carrier
AAAAA

Battleship
BBBB

Cruiser
CCC

Submarine
SSS

Destroyer
DD

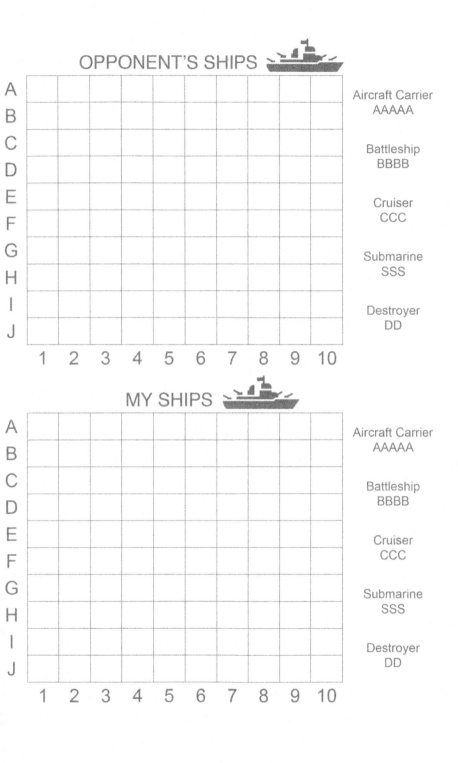

OPPONENT'S SHIPS

	1	2	3	4	5	6	7	8	9	10
A										
B										
C										
D										
E										
F										
G										
H										
I										
J										

Aircraft Carrier
AAAAA

Battleship
BBBB

Cruiser
CCC

Submarine
SSS

Destroyer
DD

MY SHIPS

	1	2	3	4	5	6	7	8	9	10
A										
B										
C										
D										
E										
F										
G										
H										
I										
J										

Aircraft Carrier
AAAAA

Battleship
BBBB

Cruiser
CCC

Submarine
SSS

Destroyer
DD

OPPONENT'S SHIPS

	1	2	3	4	5	6	7	8	9	10
A										
B										
C										
D										
E										
F										
G										
H										
I										
J										

Aircraft Carrier
AAAAA

Battleship
BBBB

Cruiser
CCC

Submarine
SSS

Destroyer
DD

MY SHIPS

	1	2	3	4	5	6	7	8	9	10
A										
B										
C										
D										
E										
F										
G										
H										
I										
J										

Aircraft Carrier
AAAAA

Battleship
BBBB

Cruiser
CCC

Submarine
SSS

Destroyer
DD

Dots and Boxes

Players: 2 to 4

The player who completes the most boxes wins.

Description

The game is played starting with a rectangular array of dots.

The two players take turns to join two adjacent dots with a horizontal or vertical line. If a player completes the fourth side of a box they initial that box and must draw another line.

When all the boxes have been completed the winner is the player who has initialled the most boxes.

PLAYER

SCORE

PLAYER

SCORE

PLAYER

SCORE

PLAYER

SCORE

PLAYER

SCORE

PLAYER

SCORE

PLAYER

SCORE

PLAYER

SCORE

PLAYER

SCORE

PLAYER

SCORE

PLAYER

SCORE

PLAYER

SCORE

PLAYER

SCORE

PLAYER

SCORE

Four in a Row

ayers: 2

e simple goal of the game is to mark four pieces in a row.
rizontal, vertical, and diagonal lines are valid.
e (X) or (O) to mark the circles.

escription

e players take turns by marking (X) or (O) in the lowest
occupied circle on the non-full columns.

e symbols then occupies the lowest unoccupied circles
that column. A player wins by placing four of their own symbols
isecutively in a line (row, column or diagonal), which ends the
ne. The game ends in a draw if the board is filled completely
:hout any player winning.

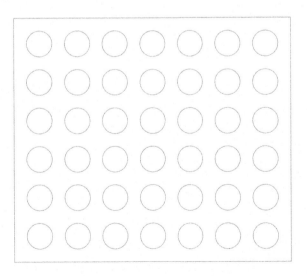

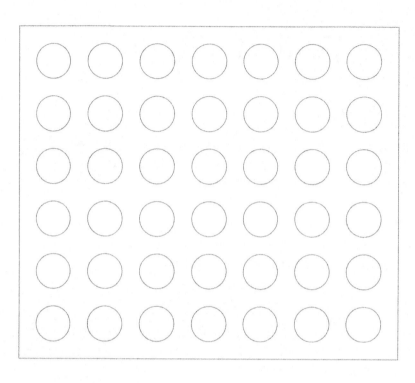

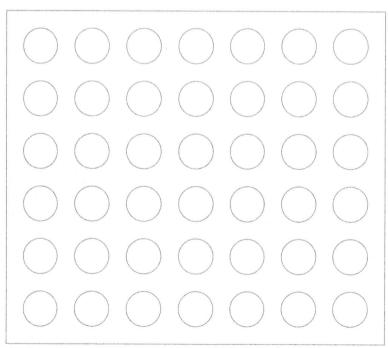

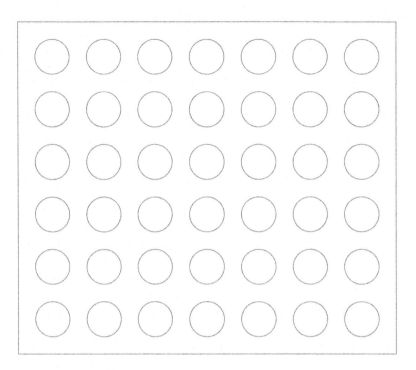

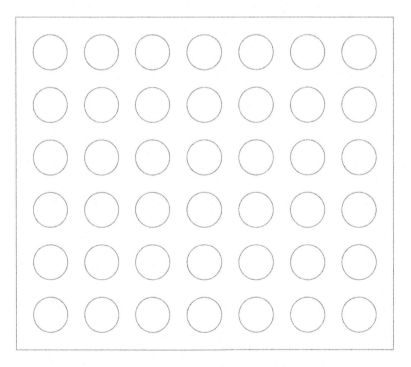

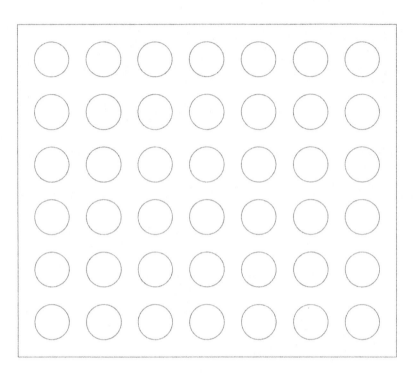

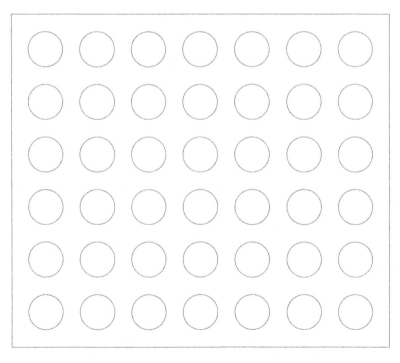

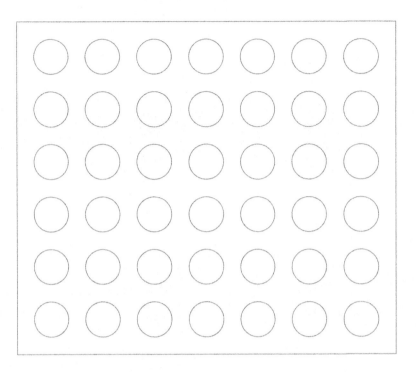

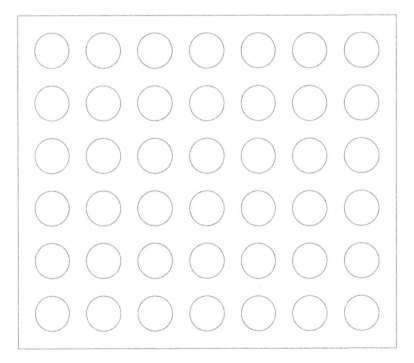

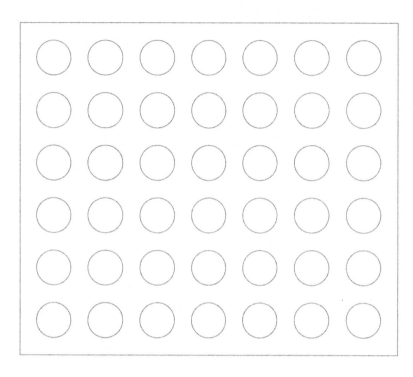

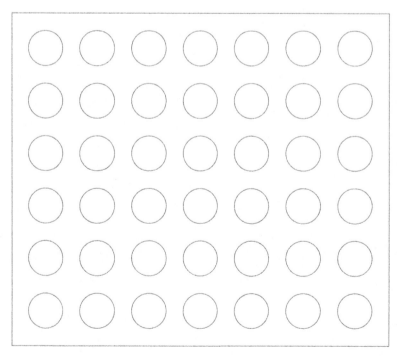

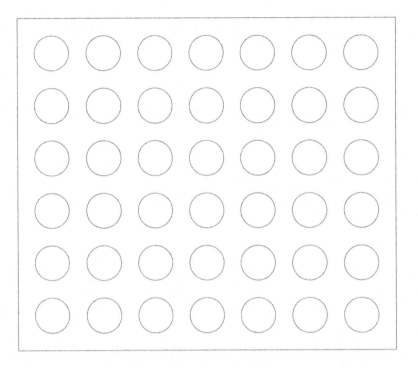

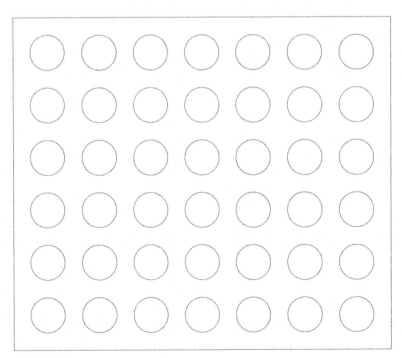

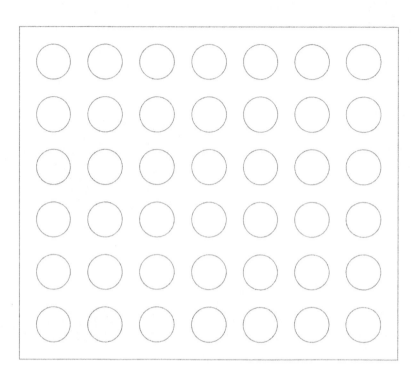

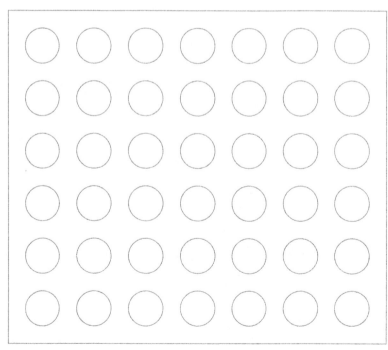

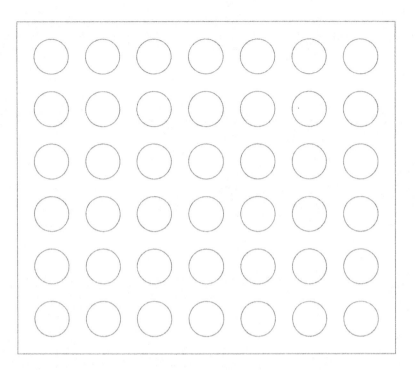

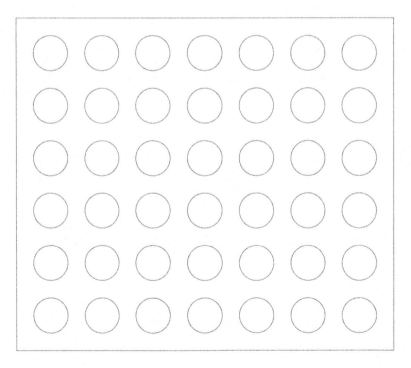

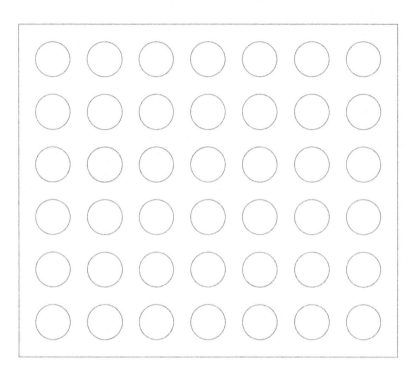

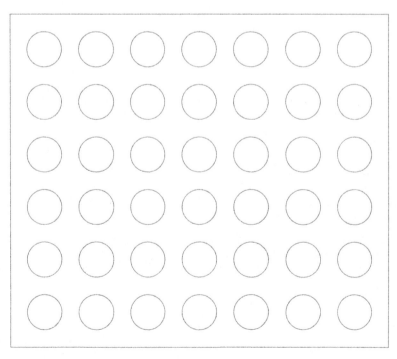

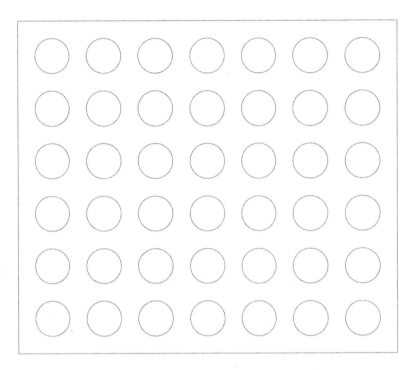

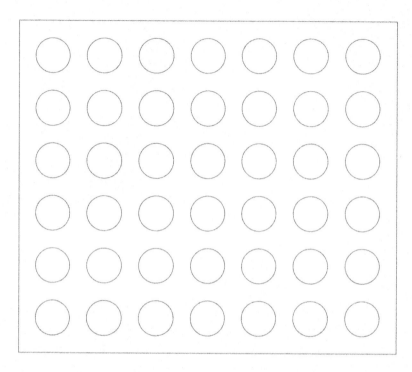

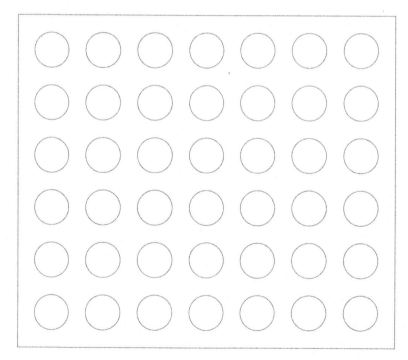

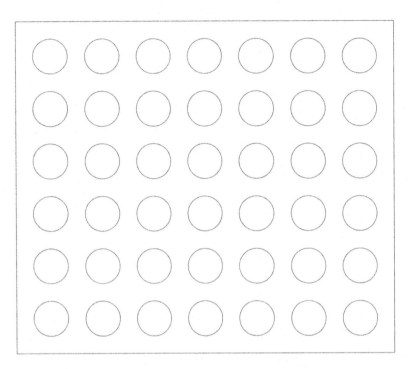

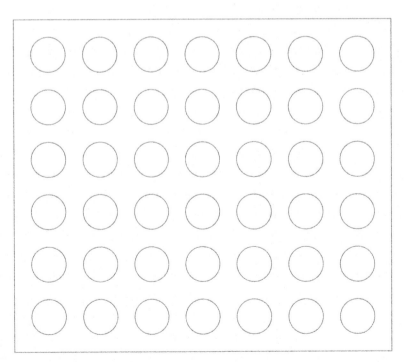

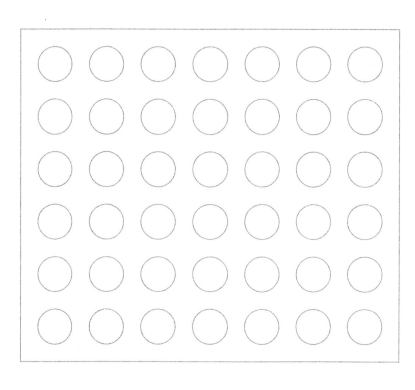

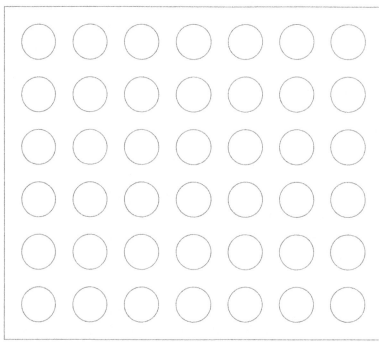

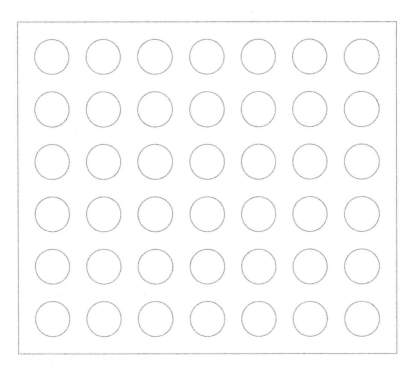

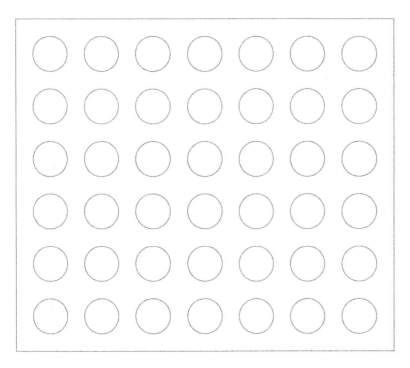

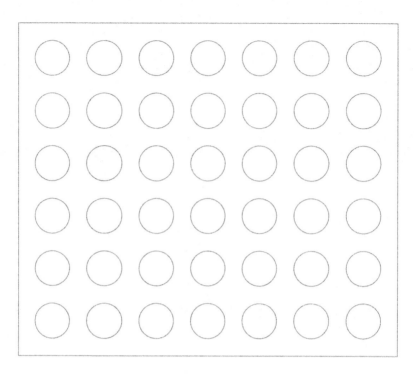

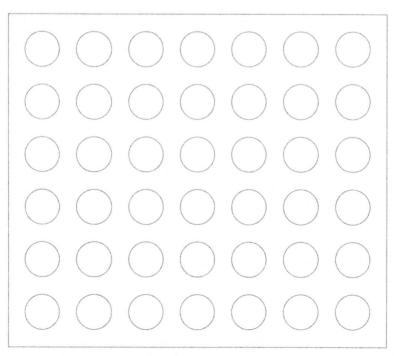

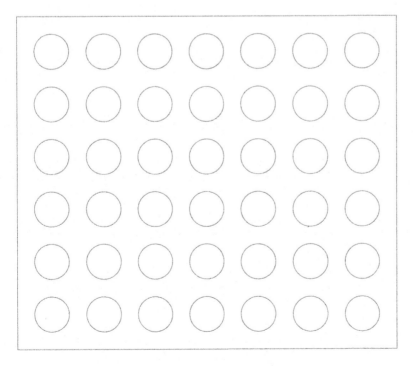

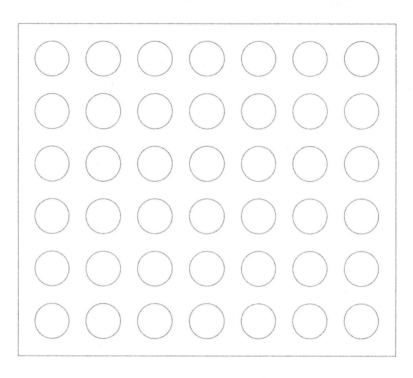

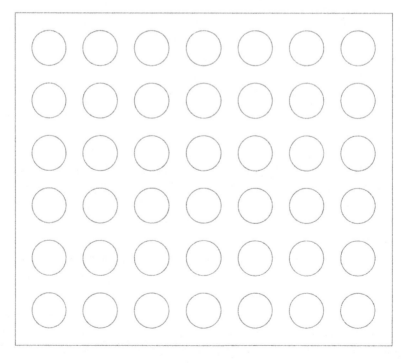

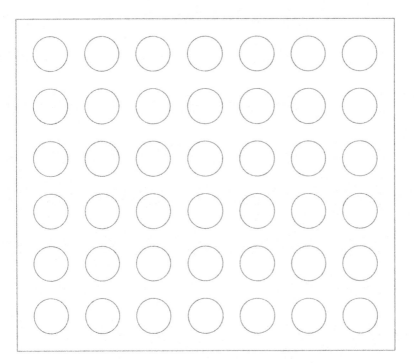

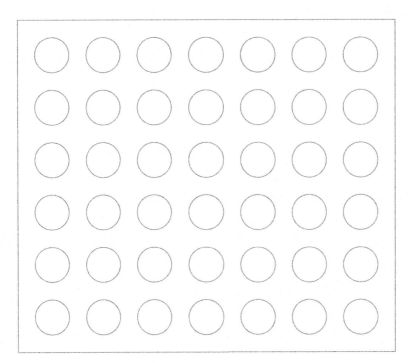

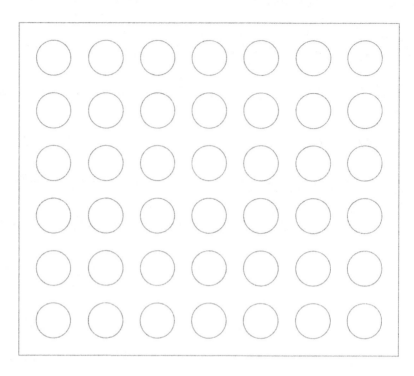

Hangman

Players: 2 to 4

Guess the word/phrase before your man gets hung!

Description

the number underlines is equivalent the number of letters on the unknown word.

As letters in the word are guessed, write them above the cooresponding underline. If a letter not in the word is guessed, complete the picture of the person each incorrect letter guess.

Most frequently, the person is drawn in 6 parts (for 6 letter guesses) in the order: head, body, left leg, right leg, left arm, right arm.

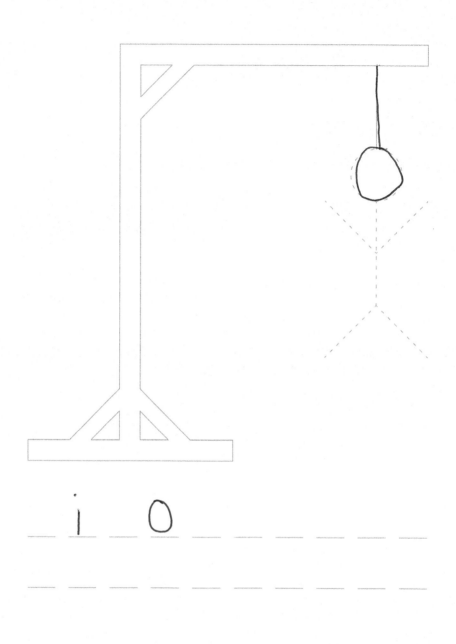

i O _ _ _ _ _

A B C D E F G H I J K L M
N O P Q R S T U V W X Y Z

DANce _ _ _ _ _

_ _ _ _ _ _ _

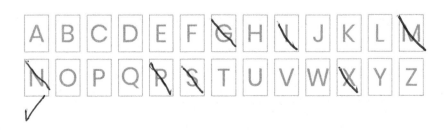

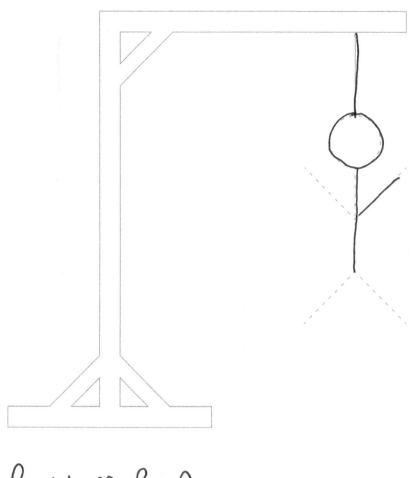

R U M B A _ _ _ _ _

_ _ _ _ _ _ _ _ _ _

A̸ B C̸ D̸ E F G̸ H I̸ J K L M
N O P Q R S T U̸ V W̸ X Y Z

B O O B i e s _ _ _ _ _

_ _ _ _ _ _ _

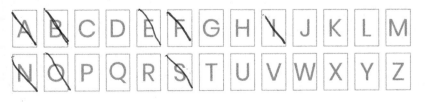

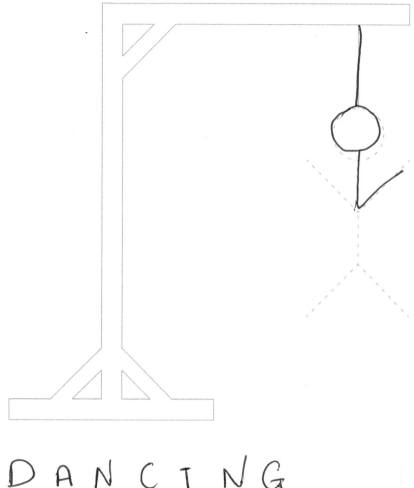

D A N C I N G _

_ _ _ _ _ _ _

A̷ B C D E̷ F G̷ H̷ I̷ J K L M
N O P Q R S T U̷ V W X Y Z

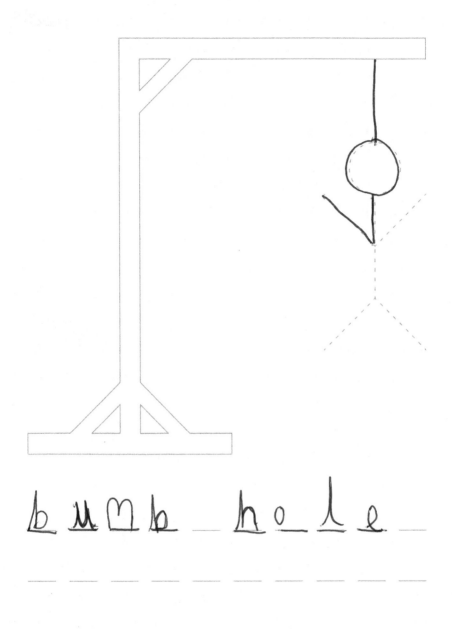

b u m b　h o l e

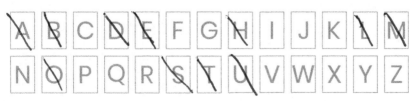

A̶ B C D̶ E̶ F G H I J K L̶ M̶
N O̶ P Q R S̶ T̶ U̶ V W X Y Z

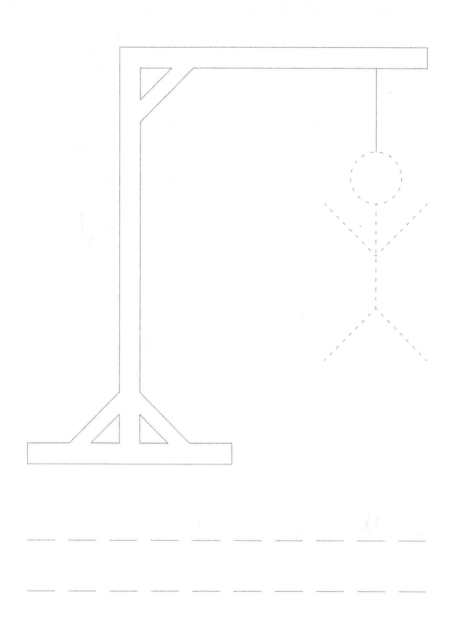

A B C D E F G H I J K L M
N O P Q R S T U V W X Y Z

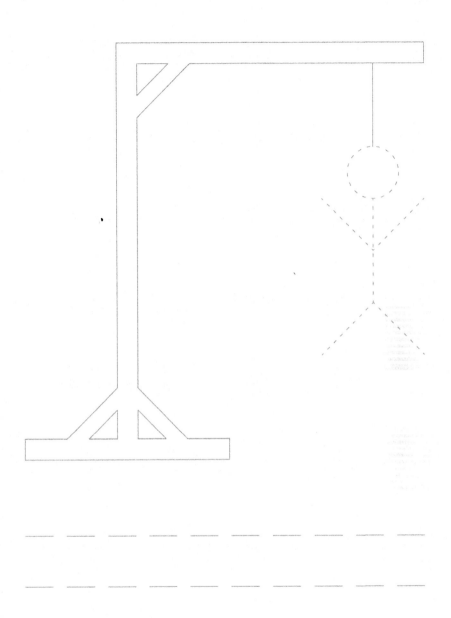

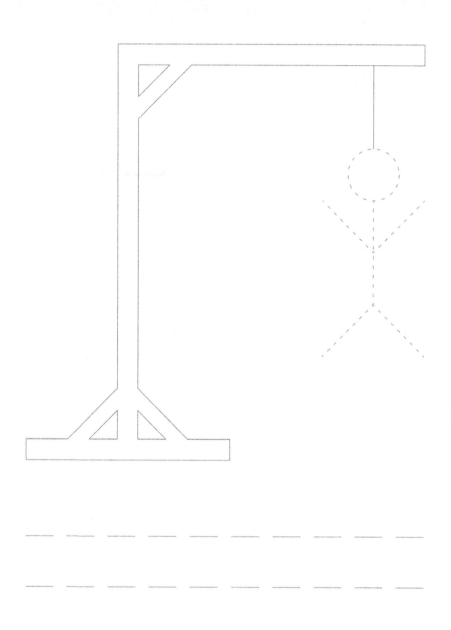

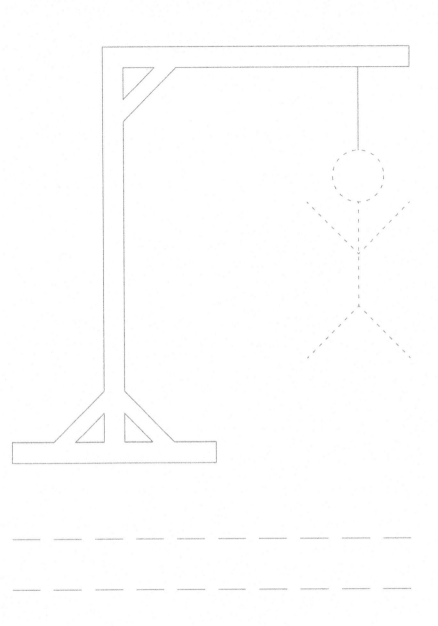

A B C D E F G H I J K L M
N O P Q R S T U V W X Y Z

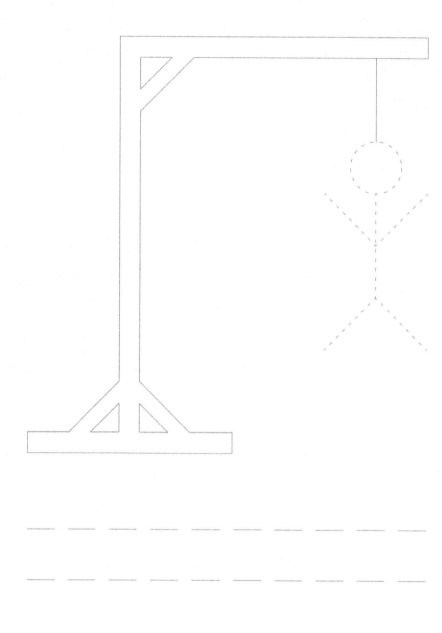

A B C D E F G H I J K L M
N O P Q R S T U V W X Y Z

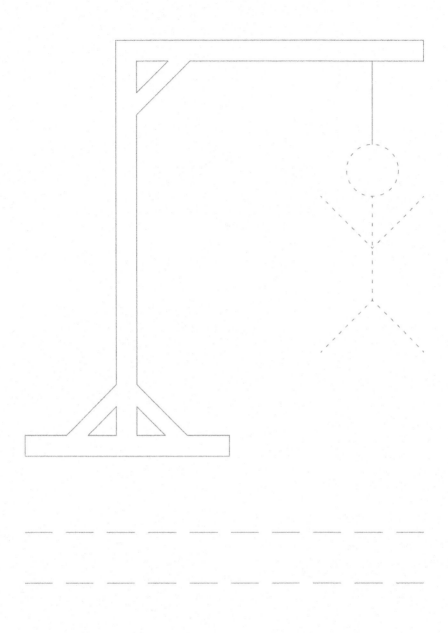

A B C D E F G H I J K L M
N O P Q R S T U V W X Y Z

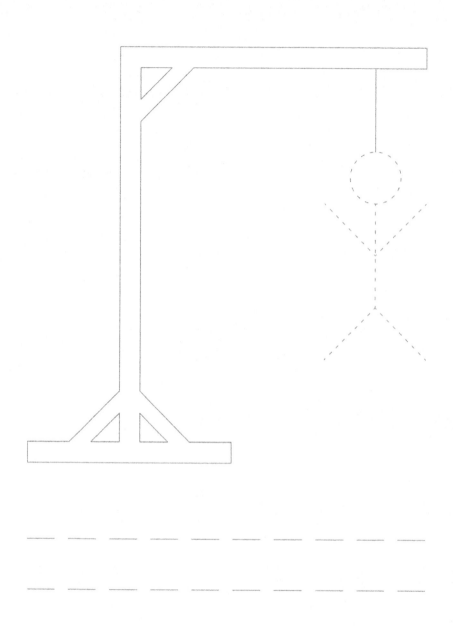

A B C D E F G H I J K L M
N O P Q R S T U V W X Y Z

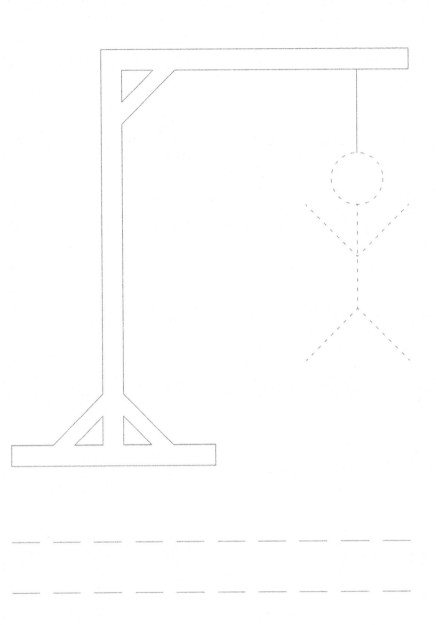

– –

– –

| A | B | C | D | E | F | G | H | I | J | K | L | M |
| N | O | P | Q | R | S | T | U | V | W | X | Y | Z |

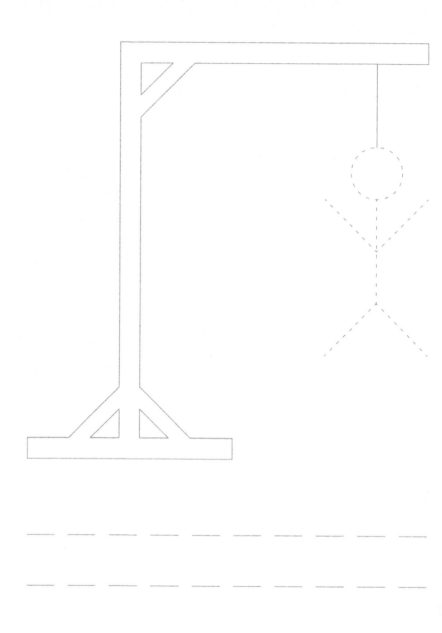

A B C D E F G H I J K L M
N O P Q R S T U V W X Y Z

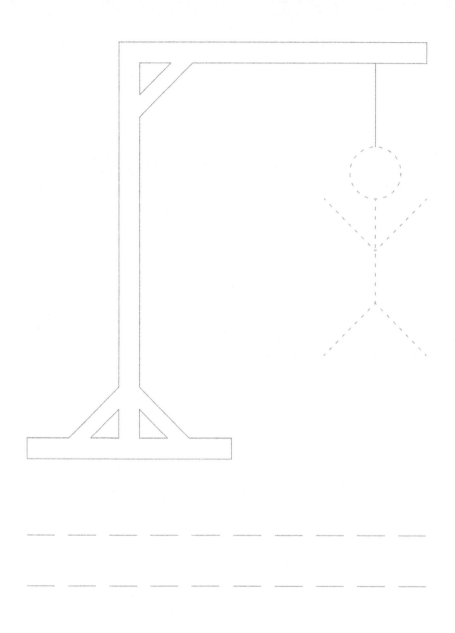

A B C D E F G H I J K L M
N O P Q R S T U V W X Y Z

Game of Sim

Players: 2

Players alternately join dots on a hexagon; the first player who competes a triangle in their own colour loses.

Description

The players take turns colouring an uncoloured line.

The first player forced to complete a triangle in their own colour loses the game.

The game cannot be a draw because there is no way to colour all the lines without creating at least one triangle.

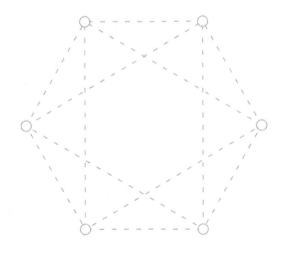

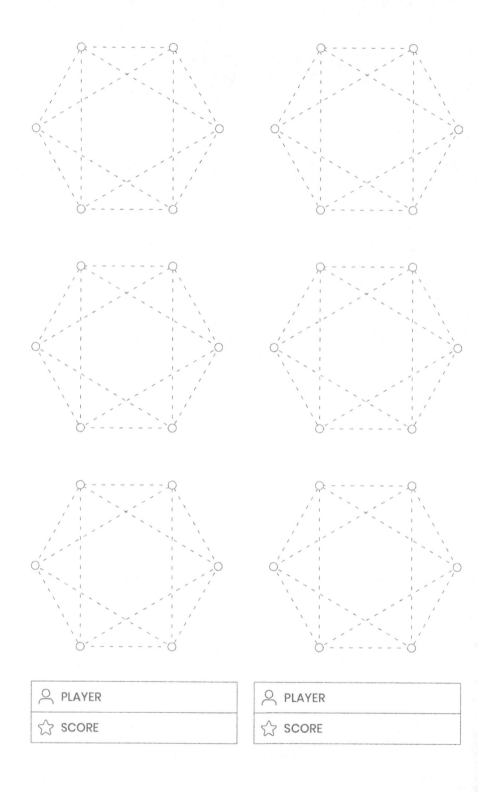

PLAYER

SCORE

PLAYER

SCORE

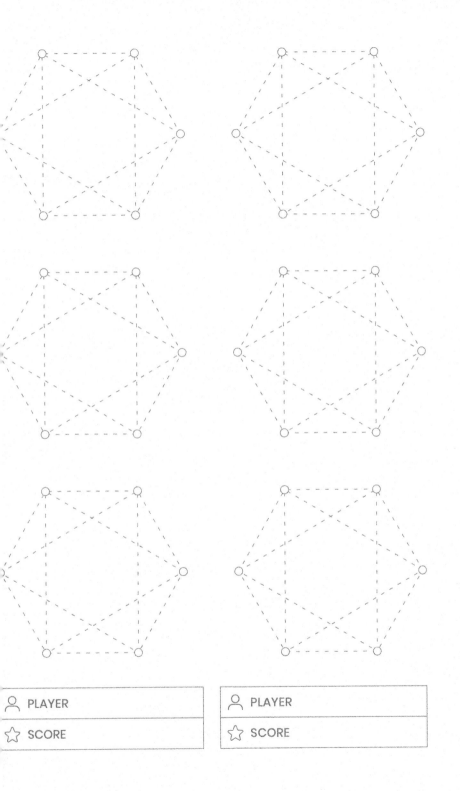

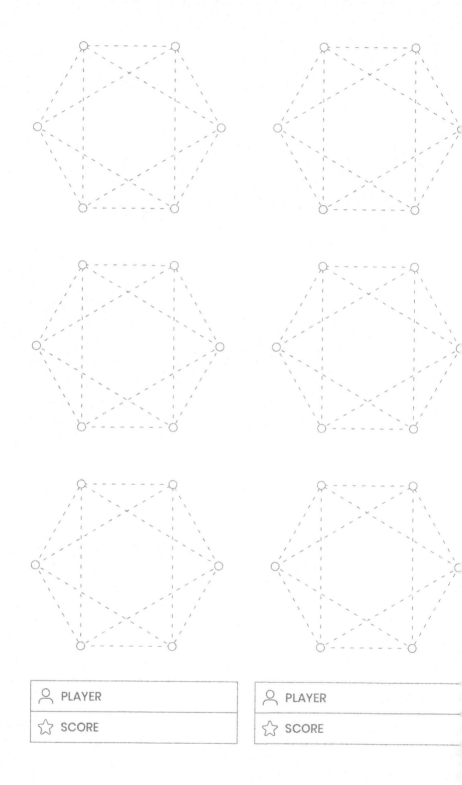

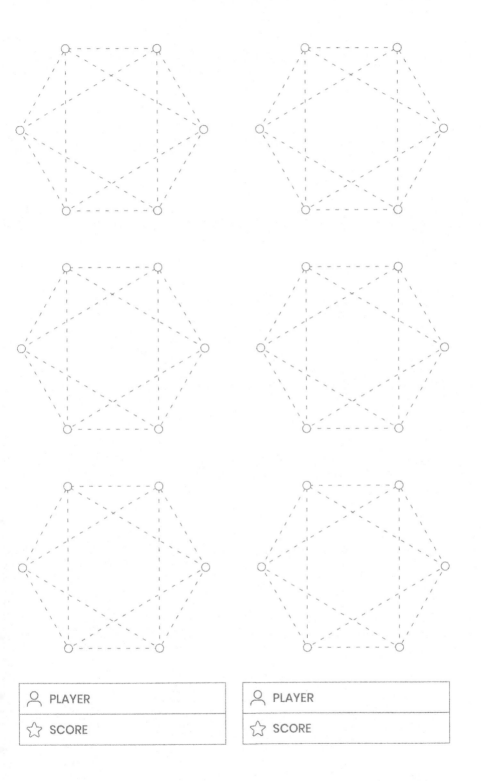

PLAYER

SCORE

PLAYER

SCORE

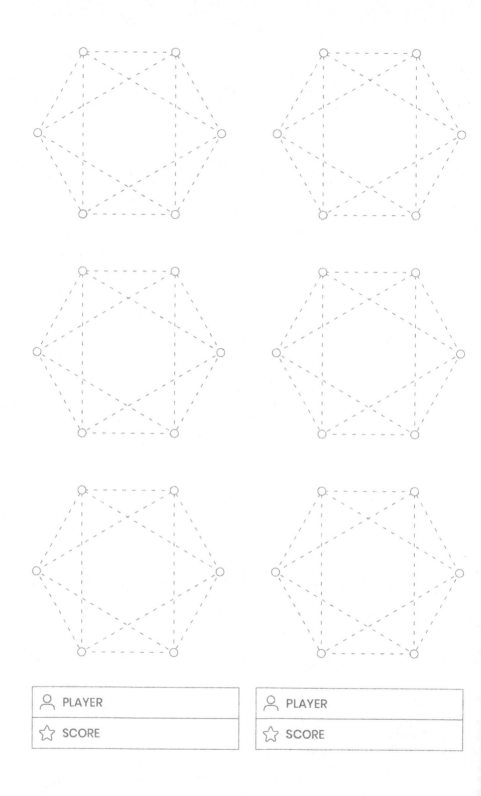

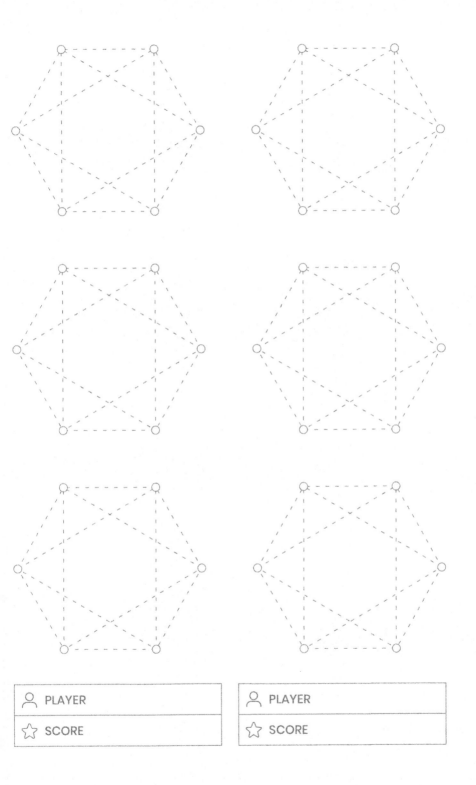

PLAYER

SCORE

PLAYER

SCORE

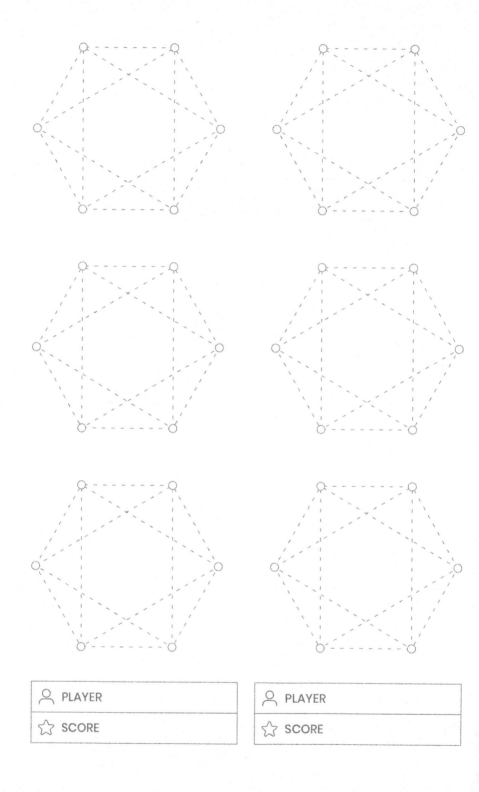

PLAYER

SCORE

PLAYER

SCORE

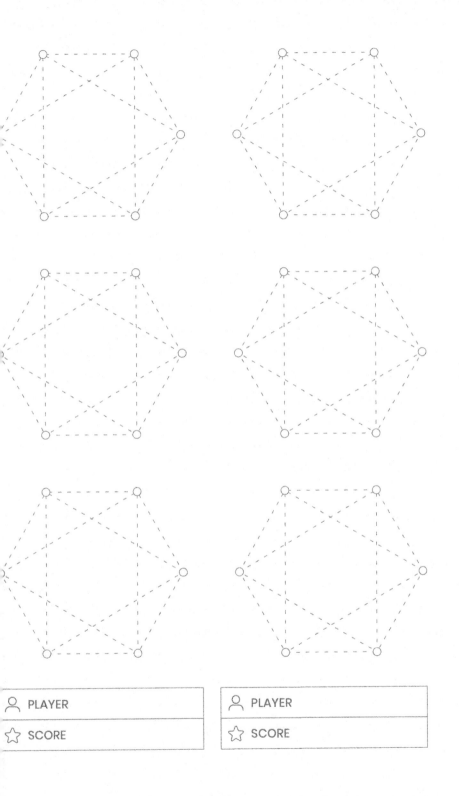

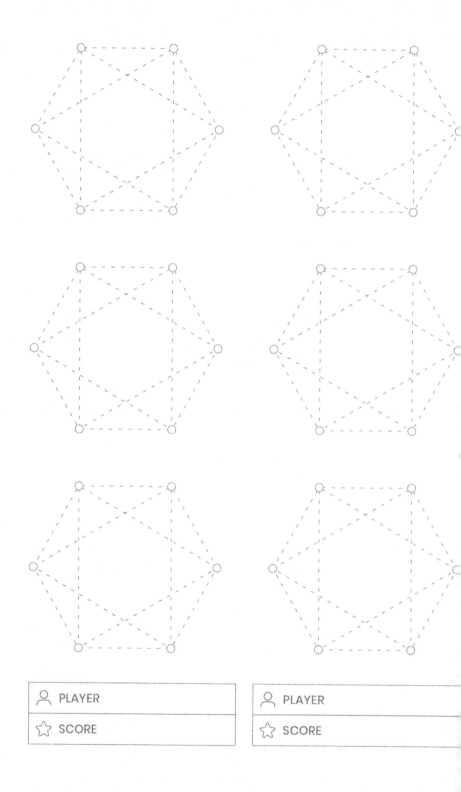

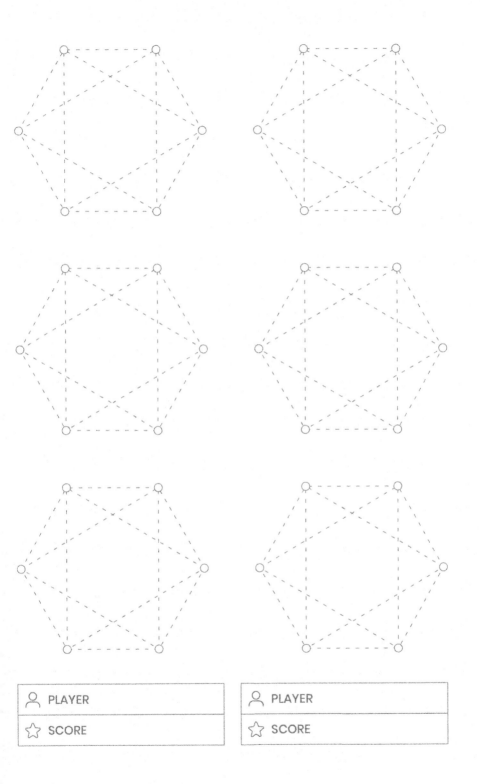

PLAYER

SCORE

PLAYER

SCORE

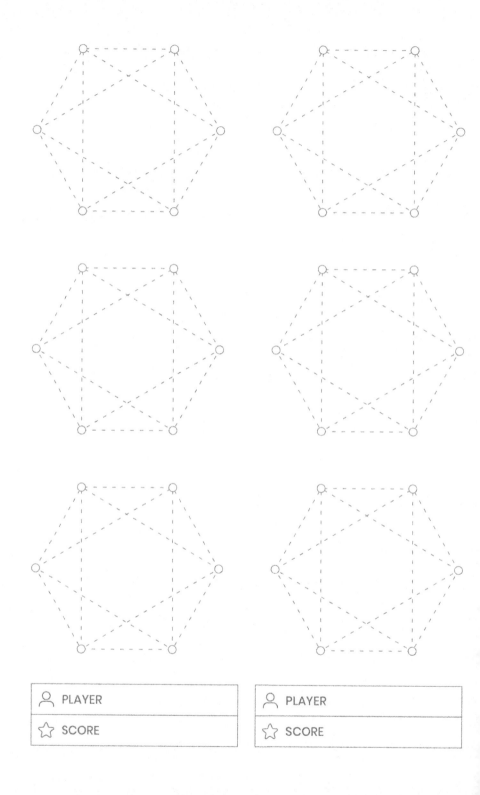

PLAYER

SCORE

PLAYER

SCORE

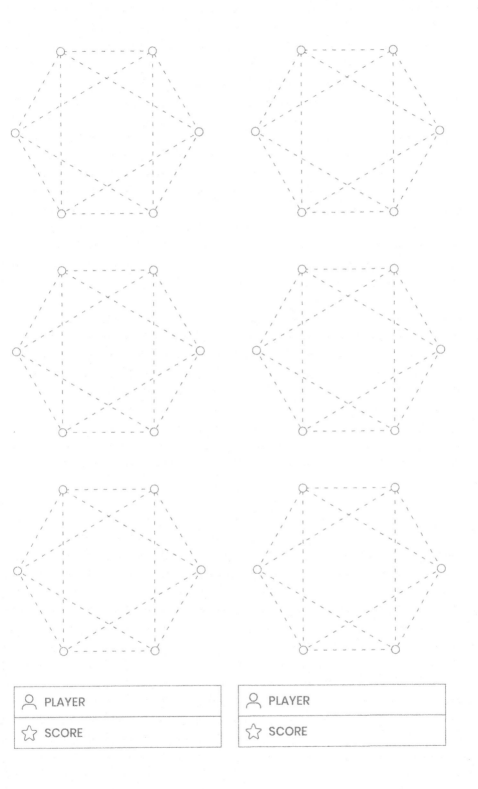

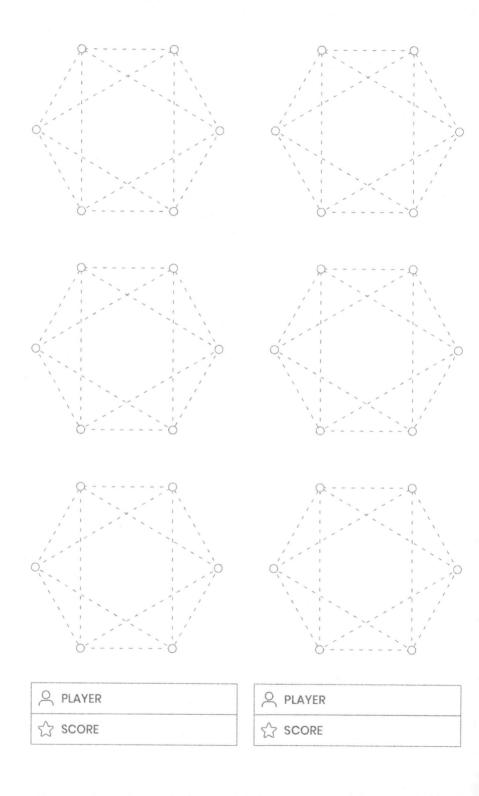

PLAYER

SCORE

PLAYER

SCORE

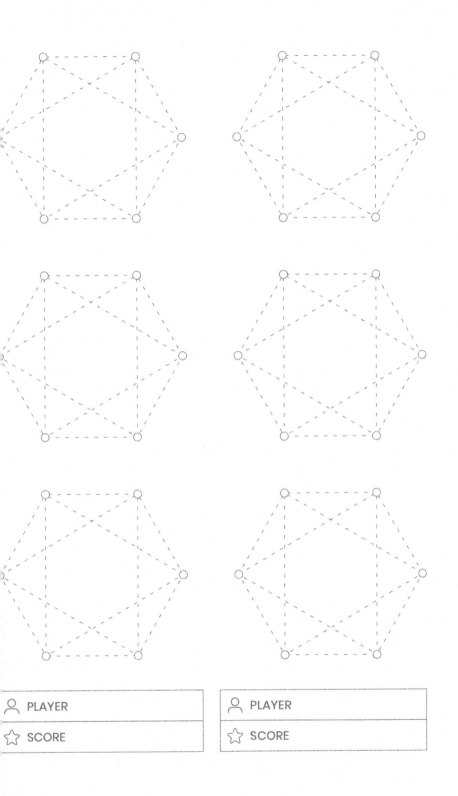

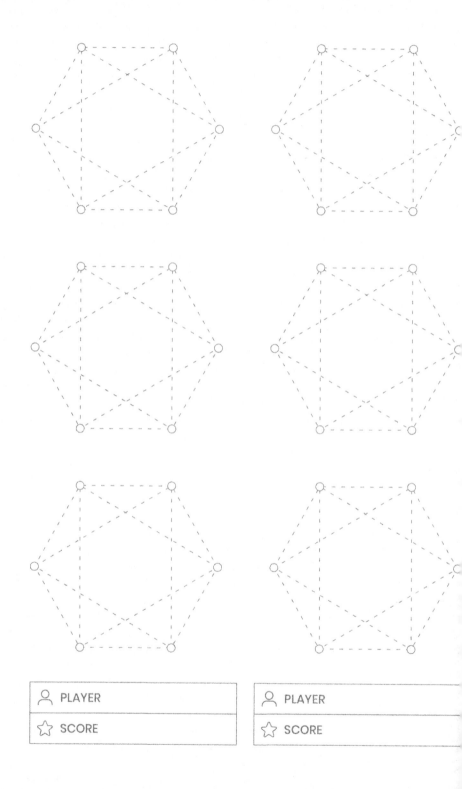

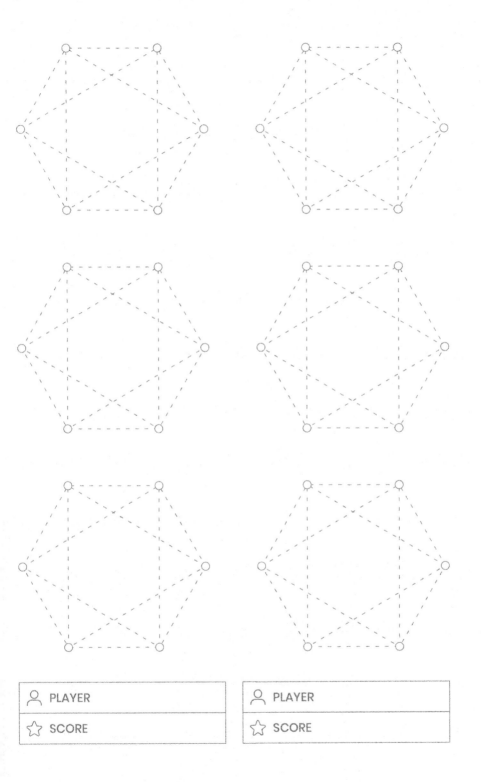

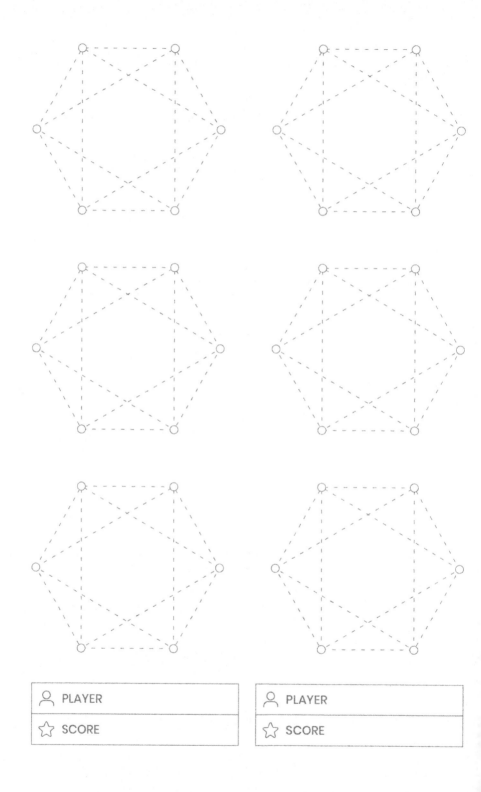

PLAYER

SCORE

PLAYER

SCORE

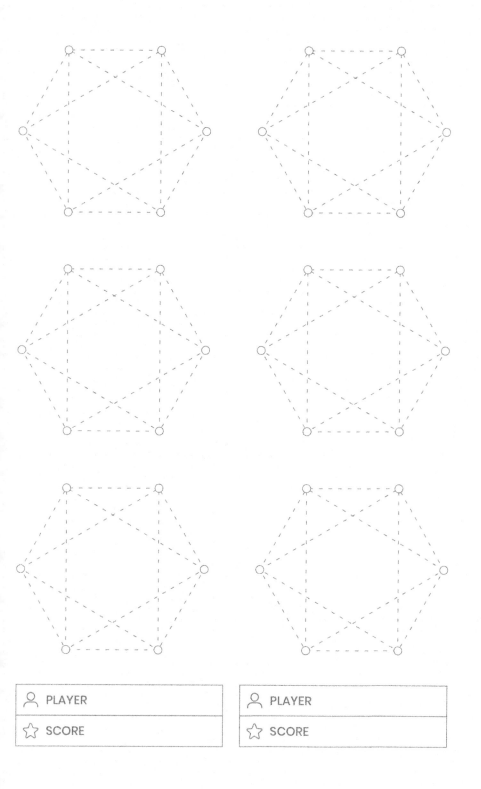

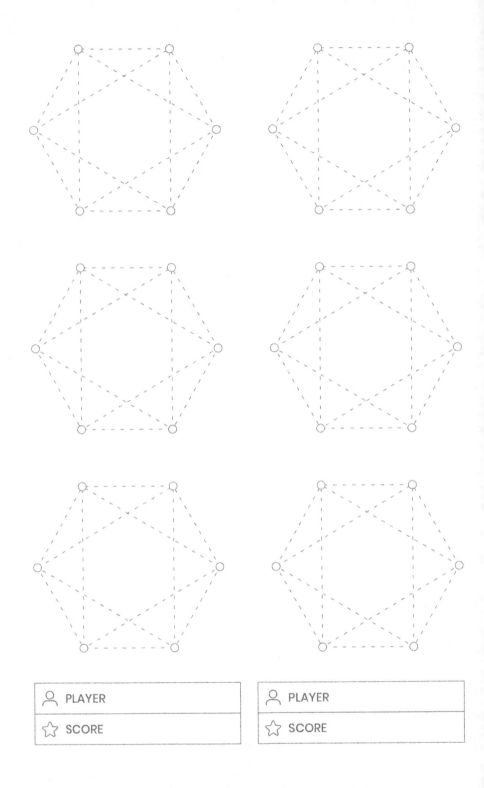

Printed in Great Britain
by Amazon

12393608R00071